YOU MUST ... THIS

1977

MILESTONES, MEMORIES,
TRIVIA AND FACTS, NEWS EVENTS,
PROMINENT PERSONALITIES &
SPORTS HIGHLIGHTS OF THE YEAR

To: Lorraine
From: Stephanie

selected and researched
by
betsy dexter

WARNER 🅦 TREASURES ™

PUBLISHED BY WARNER BOOKS

A TIME WARNER COMPANY

Warner Books, Inc.
1271 Avenue of the Americas
New York, New York 10020

Warner Treasures is a
trademark of Warner Books, Inc.

A Time Warner Company

DESIGN:
CAROL BOKUNIEWICZ DESIGN
PRINTED IN SINGAPORE
FIRST PRINTING : MAY 1995
10 9 8 7 6 5 4 3 2 1
ISBN : 0-446-91054-6

It was the year President Jimmy Carter put his stamp on the presidency. In the first of a series of initiatives, Carter pardoned draft evaders of the Vietnam War era. The decision affected some 10,000 young men. The president went on to lift travel bans to Cuba, Vietnam, Cambodia, and North Korea, and made human rights a cornerstone of his administration's foreign policy. On the environmental front, the president created a new cabinet-level agency, the **Department of Energy**. On April 18, an all-out campaign for energy conservation was begun by President Carter, who called this effort "the moral equivalent of war."

WATERGATE continued to fill the nightly news, as the Supreme Court refused to hear appeals from defendants John Ehrlichman, H. R. "Bob" Haldeman, and John Mitchell. On June 22, Mitchell became the first former attorney general to serve a prison sentence.

the son of sam

serial murder case came to a close in New York City with the arrest of David Berkowitz, 24. Berkowitz was suspected of murdering 6 people and wounding 7 over a 13-month period.

On April 30, 2,000 opponents of nuclear energy occupied the construction site of a nuclear generating plant in Seabrook, NH. By May 2, 1,414 protesters had been arrested for trespassing.

THE SPACE SHUTTLE *ENTERPRISE* SUCCESSFULLY COMPLETED SEVERAL TEST FLIGHTS AND LANDINGS.

newsreel

THE *WASHINGTON POST* ANNOUNCED THAT THE UNITED STATES WAS DEVELOPING **A NEUTRON BOMB,** DESIGNED TO KILL MASSIVE AMOUNTS OF PEOPLE WITH MINIMUM PROPERTY DAMAGE.

A 25-HOUR POWER FAILURE STRUCK NEW YORK CITY ON JULY 13, LEADING TO EXTENSIVE LOOTING AND ARSON. A TOTAL OF 3,776 LOOTERS WERE ARRESTED AND 100 POLICEMEN WERE INJURED. PROPERTY DAMAGE WAS ESTIMATED AT $135 MILLION.

international

headlines

menachem begin

became prime minister of Israel
following Yitzhak Rabin's resig-
nation as the result of a U.S.
bank fund scandal. In a major
milestone of Mideast relations,
Begin and President Anwar
Sadat of Egypt met in Israel and
then in Egypt to discuss ways to
end the Israeli-Arab conflict and
establish peace.

In Rhodesia, Prime
Minister Smith agreed
to work out a settle-
ment for Black majori-
ty rule.

IN THE WORST DISASTER IN AVIATION HISTORY, PAN AMERICAN AND KLM 747S
COLLIDED ON THE RUNWAY AT TENERIFE, IN THE CANARY ISLANDS. ALL 249 ON
THE KLM FLIGHT, AND 333 OF THE 384 ABOARD THE PAN AM JET, WERE KILLED.

In the USSR,

leonard brezhnev

replaced President Podgorny, becoming the first Soviet leader to be both Communist party chief and president. The Soviets, meanwhile, began a program of harassing and arresting political and human rights activists in the USSR, Czechoslovakia, and other Soviet bloc countries.

War broke out between the nations of Ethiopia and Somalia over a region known as Ogaden.

In Paris, normalization talks began between the United States and Vietnam. The United States agreed to stop blocking Vietnamese attempts to gain admission to the UN.

On January 17, convicted murderer Gary Gilmore was brought before a firing squad in Utah and executed. This marked the first use of capital punishment in the U.S. since 1967. Gilmore attained international attention by consistently opposing any efforts to delay his own execution. The world was fascinated by this man who claimed to welcome death.

odorono!

People began to fear their Right Guard deodorant when fluorocarbons were banned as aerosol propellants because of evidence that they harmed the ozone layer.

THE U.S. SUPREME COURT RULED THAT SPANKING OF STUDENTS BY SCHOOL OFFICIALS WAS NOT A VIOLATION OF PUPILS' CONSTITUTIONAL RIGHTS.

The FDA had a busy year. First, it recommended a ban on saccharin after tests suggested that the artificial sweetener was carcinogenic. After intense industry lobbying, the agency reversed itself and approved the sugar substitute as an over-the-counter drug.

jacqueline means

was ordained as the first female Episcopalian priest in America.

Americans in 1977 displayed a burgeoning interest in all forms of **SPIRITUALISM.** Six million citizens said they were active in transcendental meditation. Five million practiced yoga. Three million followed the Christian charismatic movement, and 2 million claimed involvement in Eastern religions.

cultural
milestones

This year saw the first national Women's Conference, the largest feminist gathering since the 1848 convention in Seneca Falls, NY. The conference drew 1,442 activists to Houston, TX. Delegates called for the ratification of the Equal Rights Amendment and the elimination of institutionalized sexual discrimination.

In Cincinnati, Larry Flynt, flamboyant country-boy publisher of *Hustler* magazine, was convicted of promoting obscenity and involvement in organized crime.

ANNIE, A MUSICAL BASED ON THE COMIC STRIP "LITTLE ORPHAN ANNIE," OPENED TO RAVE REVIEWS ON BROADWAY.

"roots," the ABC mini-series based on Alex Haley's book of the same name, proved one of the most successful shows in the history of the little screen. The program spanned an unprecedented 8 nights in a row, and reached over 80 million viewers nationwide.

television

top ten tv shows of 1977:

1. "Happy Days" (ABC)

2. "Laverne & Shirley" (ABC)

3. "ABC Monday Night Movie" (ABC)

4. "M★A★S★H" (CBS)

5. "Charlie's Angels" (ABC)

6. "The Big Event" (NBC)

7. "The Six Million Dollar Man" (ABC)

8. "ABC Sunday Night Movie" (tie) (ABC)

8. "Baretta" (tie) (ABC)

8. "One Day at a Time" (tie) (CBS)

NOTABLE WEDDINGS

Franklin D. Roosevelt, Jr., 62, presidential offspring, former New York Congressman, and foreign car salesman, married 27-year-old horsewoman **Patricia Oakes,** a socialite he met at a fox hunt. They were wed on the Roosevelt farm in Poughquag, NY, on May 6.

Senator **Jake Garn,** 44, a Utah Republican, married **Kathleen Bingham,** 27, in Salt Lake City. The bride had divorced Garn's administrative assistant a year earlier.

milestones

celeb wedding of the year

In a glittering Beverly Hills ceremony, Miss America–turned–sportscaster **PHYLLIS GEORGE,** 27, wed **ROBERT EVANS,** 46, producer of *Marathon Man* and *Chinatown.* The pair exchanged vows beneath a 400-year-old sycamore tree.

DEATHS

Milton Marx,
better known as Gummo, the unfunny Marx brother, died on April 21, at 84.

James Jones,
novelist, bestselling World War II author of *From Here to Eternity,* died on May 10

Joan Crawford,
the movie star whose maternal style was immortalized in daughter Christina's memoir, *Mommie Dearest,* died on May 10, at 69.

Vladimir Nabokov,
émigré Russian writer best known as the author of *Lolita,* died on July 2.

Elvis Presley,
the King of Rock and Roll, died with an assortment of drugs in his bloodstream at Graceland, his Memphis estate, on August 16. He was 42.

Groucho Marx,
86-year-old comedy legend, died on August 19 in New York City.

Maria Callas,
opera singer extraordinaire, died on September 16. The diva was 53.

Bing Crosby,
singer and actor, died on October 14.

James M. Cain,
novelist whose works inspired film noir classics *Double Indemnity* and *The Postman Always Rings Twice,* died on October 27.

Guy Lombardo,
bandleader, 75, best known for playing "Auld Lang Syne" every New Year, died on November 5.

Charlie Chaplin,
silent film star and comic genius, died on Christmas Day, at 88.

Howard Hawks,
director, died on December 26.

birth

ERIC BALFOUR, musician, was born April 24.

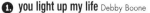

1. **you light up my life** Debby Boone
2. **best of my love** Emotions
3. **i just want to be your everything** Andy Gibb
4. **how deep is your love** The Bee Gees
5. **love theme from *a star is born* (evergreen)** Barbra Streisand
6. **sir duke** Stevie Wonder
7. **torn between two lovers** Mary MacGregor
8. **rich girl** Hall & Oates
9. ***star wars* theme/cantina band** Meco
10. **got to give it up** Marvin Gaye

hit music

debby boone's

"You Light Up My Life" stayed at the top of the charts for 10 weeks. Amazingly, no one in America seemed to know anyone who actually liked the song.

Debby Boone

12

The Sex Pistols

THIS WAS THE YEAR **THE SEX PISTOLS** BURST
INTO THE PUBLIC'S FACE, MAKING "PUNK
ROCK" A PART OF THE MUSICAL LEXICON.

fiction

1. **the thorn birds**
   colleen mccullough

2. **the silmarillion**
   j.r.r. tolkien

3. **bloodline**
   sidney sheldon

4. **scruples**
   judith krantz

5. **the holcroft covenant**
   robert ludlum

6. **illusions: the adventures of a reluctant messiah**
   richard bach

7. **the human factor**
   graham greene

8. **the honourable schoolboy**
   john le carré

9. **the women's room**
   marilyn french

10. **delta of venus: erotica**
    anais nin

It was a banner year for first-time women novelists. **Marilyn French** penned *The Women's Room,* **Maria Katzenbach** wrote *The Grab,* and **Mary Gordon** wrote *Final Payments.* The biggest success story belonged to glamorous author **Judith Krantz,** who scored a commercial triumph with her glitz-packed opus *Scruples.*

HOBBIT FANS WERE EXULTANT WITH THE PUBLICATION OF TOLKIEN'S *THE SILMARILLION,* ORIGINALLY PENNED AS A PREFACE TO *THE LORD OF THE RINGS.*

books

Vicente Aleixandre of Spain won the Nobel Prize for Literature.

In baseball, the World Series went bicoastal as the New York Yankees defeated the Los Angeles Dodgers by 4 games to 2. St. Louis Cardinal outfielder Lou Brock stole his 893rd base, breaking the record set by Ty Cobb in 1928.

IN BASKETBALL, THE PORTLAND TRAILBLAZERS PREVAILED OVER THE PHILADELPHIA 76ERS, 4 GAMES TO 2, TO SNAG THE NBA CHAMPIONSHIP.

IN FOOTBALL, THE OAKLAND RAIDERS WON THEIR FIRST SUPER BOWL CHAMPIONSHIP BY TROUNCING THE MINNESOTA VIKINGS 32–12 ON JANUARY 9 AT THE ROSE BOWL IN PASADENA.

In horse racing, 17-year-old jockey Steve Cauthen became the first jockey in history to win $6 million in purse earnings in a single year. Seattle Slew triumphed in the Kentucky Derby, the Preakness, and the Belmont Stakes to snag the Triple Crown.

sports

hit movies

1. *Star Wars* (20th Century-Fox)
   — $193,500,000
2. *Close Encounters of the Third Kind*
   (Columbia) — $82,750,000
3. *Saturday Night Fever* (Paramount)
   — $74,100,000
4. *Smokey and the Bandit* (Universal)
   — $58,949,939
5. *The Goodbye Girl* (MGM–Warner Bros.)
   — $41,839,170

Thanks to **SMOKEY AND THE BANDIT, JACKIE GLEASON** traded in his fat and irascible Brooklyn bus driver image for that of a fat and irascible Southern sheriff.

AT THE CANNES FILM FESTIVAL, *PADRE PADRONE,* A FILM DIRECTED BY ITALIAN BROTHERS PAOLO AND VITTORIO TAVIANI, BECAME THE FIRST FILM TO WIN BOTH THE GRAND PRIZE AND THE INTERNATIONAL CRITICS' PRIZE.

The success of **StarWars** signaled the beginning of a new, more polished genre of science-fiction movies. The film's phenomenal popularity came as a surprise to its producers. The space epic was originally conceived as a one-shot deal. Not until they saw theater lines stretching for several city blocks did studio executives realize that they had left the ending of the film open for a sequel. The opening crawl of the film, "Episode IV—A New Hope," was actually tacked onto the *second* release prints of the film. *Star Wars* was nominated for 10 Oscars, winning the 6 technical awards for which it was nominated.

Oscar-wise, it was a great year for films sporting feminine titles. **Annie Hall** won Best Picture, Best Actress for **Diane Keaton,** and Best Director for **Woody Allen.** *The Goodbye Girl* copped Best Actor for **Richard Dreyfuss.** *Julia* claimed Best Supporting Actor for veteran **Jason Robards** and Best Supporting Actress for **Vanessa Redgrave.**

Capitalizing on the out-of-control disco craze, John Travolta danced his way to stardom in

saturday night fever

After the film, disco was even more popular than it was before. So were white suits.

movies

top ten box-office stars

1. Sylvester Stallone
2. Barbra Streisand
3. Clint Eastwood
4. Burt Reynolds
5. Robert Redford
6. Woody Allen
7. Mel Brooks
8. Al Pacino
9. Diane Keaton
10. Robert De Niro

19

'77

The first U.S. diesel automobiles were introduced by General Motors on September 13. The Oldsmobile 88 and

cars

Oldsmobile 98 models were said to have 40 percent greater fuel efficiency than regular gasoline-powered vehicles. Driver airbags were the big news. The technology had existed for years, but Detroit was reluctant to install them.

IN THE LARGE CAR CATEGORY, *CONSUMER REPORTS* RATED THE **CHEVY CAPRICE** THE BEST BUY AT $4,901 TO $5,237. OF THE SUBCOMPACTS, THE TWO BEST BUYS WERE THE $4,145 **HONDA ACCORD** 2-DOOR HATCHBACK AND THE **HONDA CIVIC CVCC** AT $3,599.

THE EUROPEAN
INFLUENCE. FORD
GRANADA. THE SPORT
COUPE FOR 1977.
TIMELESS IN ITS
STYLING. EFFICIENT
IN ITS DESIGN. TODAY,
DISCOVER THE
RESPONSIVE
PERFORMANCE
OF THE SPORT COUPE.
COMMANDING THIS
CONTINENT AT A
PRICE FAR BELOW THE
EUROPEAN EDITION.

FORD GRANADA

FORD DIVISION

DESIGN INFLUENTIALS.
MISS ELLIETTE SCULPTS
A SENSUAL SHAPE -
BEAUTIFUL ON ANY
CONTINENT, IN THE
HALTER ALLUREMENT.
OF COURSE IT'S
NYESTA ® OF ANTRON ®
NYLON. CAPED IN
A MIST OF HAND
PAINTED CHIFFON,
$125. THE WOODWARD
SHOPS AT HUDSON'S,
MICHIGAN AND OHIO.

* A REGISTERED TRADEMARK
OF ROSELON IND

hudson's

21

The most exciting holiday jump suit has its own jacket, as LILLI ANN does it, with the most superb tailoring throughout and the most elegant details. Flame, crème, yellow and camel. For specialty shops in your area, please telephone person-to-person collect Miss Lilli Ann, San Francisco 415-863-2720.

San Francisco · Paris · London

Lilli Ann

Apparel was designed to show that women had waists, hips and thighs.

fashion

22

In makeup, "fresh" and "glowing" were the buzzwords. The natural, healthy color of the skin was In. Anything that contoured, covered up, or shaded natural skin tone was definitely Out. The thinner the makeup the better. Longer hair was back in, but haircuts had to be shaped. The hair had to glide and move. The important things were proportion and volume. Short hair was still OK, provided it was full and lustrous. The new looks in clothes revealed the shape and line of women's bodies. Apparel was designed to show that women had waists, hips and thighs. This trend reflected the new surge toward physical fitness. It was necessary for women to be in good physical shape in order to show off their bodies without FOC—Fear Of Cellulite. Well-toned, smooth stomachs were in. Items that slid, wrapped, or tied onto the body were very popular. The "half-shirt" could be seen everywhere. Swimsuits had never been more revealing.

BILL TICE creates mood dressing. Collector's choices from SWIRL. Nylon Jersey in pink, platinum and jade geometrics. The float petite, small, medium sizes $68. The wrap caftan, onesize $70. Robe Collections.

The best things come in shiny packages from Saks Fifth Avenue.

price tags

final factoid

In New York City, an amateur mountain climber named George Willig scaled the 1,350-foot South Tower of the World Trade Center.

archive photos: inside front cover, pages 1, 5, 7, 15, inside back cover.

associated press: pages 2, 3, 4, 17, 25.

photofest: pages 8, 9, 10, 12, 13, 18, 19.

photo research:
alice albert

coordination:
rustyn birch

design:
carol bokuniewicz design
mutsumi hyuga

'77